Hardwick's Services Limited, Scarborough

A Wallace Arnold country bus company from 1952 to 1987

Stuart Emmett

Text © Stuart Emmett, 2020.
First published in the United Kingdom, 2020,
by Stenlake Publishing Ltd.,
54-58 Mill Square, Catrine, Ayrshire,
KA5 6RD.

Telephone: 01290 551122
www.stenlake.co.uk

ISBN 9781840338607

Printed by Blissetts,
Roslin Road,
Acton,
W3 8DH

Picture Acknowledgements

Unless stated below, the pictures are from my own collection of our family pictures and from other sources. For the latter, where the original photographer cannot be traced, I offer my apologies for the lack of accreditation and would be pleased to be able to correct this in future editions.

Busphotos.co.uk: pages 18, 39 (upper)
John Cockshott Archive (Transport Library): page 26
Mike Davies: pages 41 (lower), inside back cover
John Kaye: page 16
Leeds Transport Historical Society: page 17

Peter Hirst/Mineralcraft: pages 43, 44
Omnibus Society Archive: pages 20, 30
PM Photography: pages 7, 8, 11, 12 (lower), 14, 15, 19 (lower), 21, 22, 28, 31, 33, 35

Sources

Brown, Stewart J; 1996, *Holidays by Coach*
Barber, S & Davies, R; 2007, *Glory Days: Wallace Arnold*
Barber, S & Davies.R; 2010, Wallace Arnold Days
David Slater at http://www.ipernity.com/doc/davidslater-spoddendale/36746818/in/album/751954
Heming B and Little D; 1989, Bus Handbook, 3 Yorkshire
Jenkinson, Keith; 1992, East Yorkshire Motor Services Ltd ('Twixt, Wold, Carr & Coast)
The PSV Circle, Wallace Arnold Tours, Supplement P73 dated June 1956
The PSV Circle, Wallace Arnold Tours, Publication P73R dated October 1966
The PSV Circle/The Omnibus Society, Wallace Arnold Tours, Part 1, 1919 to 1957, Fleet History PB15 dated July 1979
The PSV Circle/The Omnibus Society, Wallace Arnold Tours, Part 2, 1958 to 1979, Fleet History PB15 dated May 1979
The PSV Circle/East Yorkshire Motor Services Ltd, Part 1 (1926 to 1987) dated April 2018

And discussions on the Old Bus Photos website and on various Facebook sites from people like Tony Walshaw, Michael Davies, Keith Easton, John Darwent, Steve Adamson and many others for updates, corrections and general assistance.

Introduction

This book concentrates on the rural operator Hardwick's of Scarborough, a delightful country bus operation, owned in its later years by Wallace Arnold Tours (WAT) who also possessed two other Leeds-based stage companies, Farsley and Kippax, urban operations that are better known by enthusiasts. The more remote coastal Hardwick's operations were not only the first but also the last of the three Wallace Arnold Tours stage bus companies (the other two operations are covered in another book in this series).

To put Wallace Arnold's stage operations into perspective, the following is a summary using data from 1966:

- Hardwick's hourly service was effectively one main 15-mile rural route from Scarborough to Ebberston and had three double-deckers and four single-deckers. They carried up to 480,000 passengers a year and operated from 1952 to 1987.

- Farsley Omnibus Co. Ltd., Richardshaw Lane, Stanningley had a 7-mile intensive 15/30 min headway urban route on the western outskirts of Leeds between Pudsey and Horsforth via Farsley and Rodley. They had six double-deckers, carrying up to 2.3m passengers a year, and ran under Wallace Arnold Tours control from 1952 to 1968.

- Kippax and District Motor Co. Ltd., Butt Hill, Kippax, ran from Leeds to Ledston Luck, via Cross Gates, Garforth and Kippax on the Eastern outskirts of Leeds. The hourly service operated with six double-deckers carrying up to 1.4m passengers a year on the 11-mile route, and ran under WAT control from 1956 to 1968.

The History to 1952

David Hardwick from Snainton founded Hardwick's in 1922 as Snainton Hardwick's Services. The garage was in Snainton and located on a small side road off the A170 from Scarborough to Pickering and Thirsk. It latterly had a heightened roof section to take double-deckers, with lower height doors on either side for the single-deck vehicles. The garage was still there in 2017 and was used latterly by a car restoration company for storage.

At the age of 76 in 1947, David Hardwick retired and sold the company to a Hull coal merchant, Rafferty and Watson who went on to buy out the Willing's share of Willing's and Noble trading as Forge Valley Services, (who were also known as the Blue Bus Service). Forge Valley ran from Langdale End and Hackness into Scarborough daily in the summer and in winter, on Monday/Thursday and Saturday. They also ran a daily service from Hutton Bascal and Ayton to Scarborough. The Hutton Bascal route was incorporated into the Hardwick's service whilst the Hackness route, that had remained with Noble, ran until July 1961, when they sold out to United Automobile Services.

An early Hardwick's bus, very likely in the 1920s, especially judging by the "Roaring Twenties" dressed lady on the right.

Within a few years, Rafferty and Watson, the new owners of Hardwick's, realised the bus business was not compatible with their coal business, so in March 1952 they sold Hardwick's to Wallace Arnold (formed in 1926 by Wallace Cunningham and Arnold Crowe).

Wallace Arnold already had an excursion and tours operation in Scarborough which had come about after the Second World War, when they had started to rebuild the company. Many coaches had been requisitioned by the Ministry of Defence and most of those returned were not in good shape. Additionally, with the increased demand for leisure travel, the existing bus manufacturers struggled to cope, leading to long delivery times for new buses. Many operators looked to rebuild and refurbish older vehicles. As part of this policy, WAT bought a Leeds company, Wilks & Meade, so that the post-war re-building of their fleet could be handled inhouse.

With the fleet now being managed, company rebuilding was now about expansion of the business. Consequently, in 1945 WAT's first purchases out of the West Riding of Yorkshire involved four small Scarborough companies with four coaches coming from Barker, Horsley, Fletcher's Coaches and Pullman Motors. These Scarborough purchases now enabled WAT to be ready for the perceived post-war growth for coastal traffic, (indeed two years later WAT bought Waverley Motor Coach Tours in Paignton, Devon).

In 1946 all the purchased Scarborough companies were consolidated into Barkers. Expansion in 1947 involved twelve new Bedford OBs for Scarborough; eleven with Duple bodies that had been ordered by Barkers but were now registered in Leeds as KUA181-190 and 510, and another one, (KUB745) that was bodied by Plaxton. Additionally, transferred to Barkers in 1947 was another Bedford OB with Plaxton FC30F body (KNW902) new in 1946, and it stayed with Barkers until October 1949. KUM83, a 1947 Bedford/Duple OB, was also transferred in 1948 and there were other transfers to Scarborough too.

In May 1947 another Scarborough company, Rawlings, was bought. This purchase included their Columbus Ravine premises along with three 1946 Plaxton-bodied Commers, initially licensed to Barkers; in October 1949 this licence was finally transferred to WAT.

Noble, trading as Forge Valley Motors, Bedford OWB CPY 556 in its grey and blue livery makes its way out of Scarborough to Hackness. They sold out to United Automobile Services in 1961.

A 1930s picture of Rawlings trucks/charabancs outside Columbus Ravine Depot that was later rebuilt by Wallace Arnold.

Wallace Arnold's depot in Columbus Ravine in the early 1950s. From left to right is GUA829, a 1938 Leyland TS8/Duple; KUB477, a 1947 Bedford OB/Duple; next is one of the three Commer Commandos ex-Rawlings of Scarborough in 1947 which were registered CVN240 to 242. Next is an unidentified Daimler and the other two ex-Rawlings Commers.

The purchase of Hardwick's in 1952 enabled synergies with the WAT Scarborough coach activities with fourteen vehicles coming with the Hardwick's operation. WAT immediately sold off a Dennis from 1938 and five Bedfords (a WTB, three OWBs and an OB); and retained eight, these being seven Bedford OBs and one Commer. These ran for a few more years, with the Commer staying until 1960.

GPY645 was the longest surviving original Hardwick's vehicle that was new in 1950. It stayed with WAT Hardwick's from 1952 until 1960 and looks here to have the WAT cream and red livery, along with the Wallace Arnold crest on the side.

Hardwick's routes

From the Snainton depot, Hardwick's ran their service easterly from nearby Ebberston into Scarborough, a distance of 15 miles and with a 12-mile market day south-westerly service from Ebberston to Malton.

The routes in 1954 from Scarborough (Victoria Road) were:

• Daily to Ebberston (The Nook)
• Thursday, Saturday and Sunday to Sawdon (Council Houses)
• Saturday to North Moor (Wykeham Forestry House)
• Thursday, Saturday and Sunday to Yedingham
• Saturday to Malton (Market Place)

Effectively this was virtually one route to Ebberston and by 1978 the daily service to Ebberston had a Thursday and Saturday diversion to Sawdon. On Saturday there was also a 12-mile extension from Ebberston to Yedingham and Malton. The former once a week spur off to North Moor and the shorts to Yedingham were abandoned sometime between 1967 and 1978.

The basic service to Ebberston took 40 minutes and required two vehicles. There were thirteen journeys on Monday to Saturday (with three shorts to Stainton or Sawdon), and seven journeys on a Sunday. Buses left Scarborough at 10 minutes past the hour and returned from Ebberston at 50 minutes past the hour; this involved an immediate timetabled arrival and departure time from Ebberston, giving a long 40 minute layover in Scarborough. The immediate turnaround in Ebberston was probably due to the road layout there and the associated access roads, as the buses came from Snainton on the main A170 top road and turned left into Ebberston on Main Street that ran down the hill towards the bottom of the village. There the buses turned left onto the bottom road (the B1258) back to Snainton. So, this was effectively a 12 minute circular route from Snainton out to Ebberston on the top road, and back on the bottom road to Snainton.

909EUM came from Farsley in March 1968 and was exchanged for Reliance 9206NW as Farsley was converting to pay as you enter operation. Seen here at the end of its country run at the Ebberston terminus, (and it must have arrived early and did not make an immediate arrival/departure), it was the first bus in July 1966, whilst with the WAT Farsley operation, to receive this more cream version of the livery.

The intermediate route timings from Scarborough were:

- Seamer 13 minutes
- Ayton 17 minutes
- Wykeham 23 minutes
- Ruston 27 minutes
- Brompton 30 minutes
- (Sawdon 38 minutes with one journey on a Thursday and two on a Saturday)
- Snainton 34 minutes
- Ebberston 40 minutes

The detail for the extended two journeys on a Saturday from Scarborough to Malton was:

- Yedingham 55 minutes
- Rillington 70 minutes
- Malton 85 minutes

At Malton, the arriving bus laid over for 90 minutes before returning and passengers in either direction would change buses in Snainton with the normal Ebberston service.

9203NW on "Pay as you Enter" duty.

Hardwick's also undertook other "unusual" operations and when researching this book, the following story was sent to me: 'A little detail that I doubt is well-known was an extra service provided by Hardwick's. In the 1970s I was working in banking at Scarborough. Every Thursday, a Hardwick's driver called at the bank with another employee to pay in the bus company's takings for the week. He would also be carrying about four tiers of fresh eggs from a local Ebberston farm. Most of the bank staff ordered their eggs the week previously and brought their cartons to work pending the arrival of the eggs which would be placed in a side room for cartons to be filled as and when. The chief cashier would pay the driver and collect the money from the staff. Great days!' They also were "parcel" carriers as told in another story: 'In 1952 my parents bought a Silver Cross pram. When it arrived at the shop in Scarborough, it was taken and put on the bus for my father waiting at the stop in Snainton.'

The public support for Hardwick's was legendary with few using the parallel United service; therefore, in the days of few people having cars, Hardwick's loadings were impressive. Hardwick's service had not been extended beyond Ebberston to Pickering on the A170, as United Automobile held the licence for a Scarborough-Ebberston-Pickering-Helmsley-Thirsk to Ripon service numbered 128. However, after deregulation in 1986, Hardwick's was to extend to Pickering on route 128, which by this time, had been truncated to operate to Helmsley.

WAT GWX74 on excursion duty for Oliver's Mount in Scarborough. The Bedford Duple OB was new to McDonald, Stanley, Wakefield in August 1948 and came to WAT in 1949 and stayed until 1954. In the 1960s the two double-deckers ran alternate journeys all day. In the morning peak duplicates were needed and the spare double-decker (MUM275) and three single-deckers were used. At Scarborough during the day, two of the three single-deckers did schools contracts to playing fields/swimming baths and also worked for the WAT Scarborough depot on local excursions, such as to Oliver's Mount.

A stalwart of the fleet from 1953 until the start of one manning for pay as you enter operations in 1967, RUA294 is seen in Newham's Garage Scarborough terminus complete with the original script front upper deck fleet name and the WAT crest on the side. In the evening peak, the spare Hardwick's double-decker left as a duplicate on the 1610 hours journey and the three single-deckers came back with the 1710 service bus. The same passengers tended to use the same bus or duplicate bus every day as told in another story sent to me: 'In the 1960s on the the 16.xx departure, the spare double-deck duplicate operated to Seamer via Racecourse Road on the A174 in Scarborough rather than via the service route to Seamer roundabout, although of course it could not pick up or set down passengers whilst on that route. However, it carried the evening papers to newsagents en route, and these were chucked off the back platform by the conductor. A typical country bus service in the best sense of the word!'

MUM275 reverses into Newham's Garage, with a 92xxNW Plaxton inside. The original terminus in Scarborough for a few years was at Castlehouse and Vaseys Garage in St. Thomas Street, but they soon moved to Newham Garage at 56 Victoria Road, where they were to remain until 1967. Vehicles approached the garage along Victoria Road then swung left into Cambridge Street before reversing straight back into the garage in a tight manoeuvre.

HNW365D at Northway with an early Bristol RE type bus of West Yorkshire behind for Bradford. This was an important West Yorkshire route that ran from Bradford, Leeds, York, Malton to Scarborough, with two trips per day from Bradford (taking 3 hours 40 mins), plus eleven extra trips from Leeds (3 hours), thirteen extra trips from York (1 hour 45 mins) and four extra trips from Malton (1 hour), giving from Malton to Scarborough 30 trips a day.

Due to increases in charges at Newham's terminus in Scarborough, Hardwick's moved in March 1967 to the 1939-built West Yorkshire Bus Station in Northway.

All Leyland SUA296 from 1954 has just left the West Yorkshire Northway Scarborough bus station that was used for a short time in 1967. Northway operated as a one way system and vehicles either entered through the garage doors (on the right in the picture) or via the middle entrance to the stands (behind the lamp post in the picture). They exited through Brook Street and then Trafalgar Street (just out of view on the left of the picture).

Northway terminus was short-lived and later in 1967 (also reported as 27th April 1969) Hardwick's terminus moved to the Westwood Coach Station where it stayed until 1982. Westwood had been opened in May 1954, but in 1970 East Yorkshire Motor Services moved to the United Automobile Services Valley Bridge bus station. The only stage bus service then left at Westwood was Hardwick's. Westwood was also used as a bus park and for some express services. It was closed in 1982 (also reported as 23rd September 1984), so Hardwick's moved across town to the Wallace Arnold depot at Columbus Ravine and started their service from opposite the depot.

The Fleet

Hardwick's vehicles were garaged and cleaned at Snainton where minor repairs were also done. All major work took place at Wallace Arnold's workshop in Beconsfield Street, Scarborough or, at the central workshop in Leeds.

On acquiring Hardwick's, Wallace Arnold clearly thought investment was needed and two new Leyland double-deckers were soon ordered. These buses would be the mainstay of the operation until one-man operations started in the mid-1960s. Meanwhile, until these arrived, Wallace Arnold placed two ex-Leeds pre-war AEC Regents at Hardwick's and additionally transferred two coaches to Hardwick's to replace some of the inherited Bedford OB buses.

AUM404 was new in 1935 and bought from Leeds City Transport by WAT in 1950 for contract work. It came to Hardwick's in October 1952 where it stayed until 1954 when SUA296 was delivered. It is likely seen parked at Sawdon.

AUM404 is now in full WAT red and cream stage bus livery. After its time with Hardwick's, it returned to WAT for schools' contract work at Royston and finally spent a month with Farsley in 1956 before its withdrawal. The high placed rear indicator was so that the original owners Leeds City Transport could show a full advertisement.

AUM433, an AEC Regent with Roe H30/26R body was new as Leeds City Transport 190 in June 1935. This was one of seven that was rebuilt in 1948/1949 by East Lancs (Bridlington) and was one of two which were withdrawn in late 1950 whilst the balance five were stored (and reappeared in 1954 on tramway replacement work). After withdrawal at Leeds, 433 passed to Wallace Arnold in June 1951 and saw service with Hardwick's from June 1952 until the end of 1955 and the arrival of MUM275. 433 then returned to Leeds for disposal and is seen here in 1956 at Wallace Arnold's Sayner Road Garage in Leeds.

DUB926 was another WAT purchase from Leeds City Transport and was a 1936 Leyland TD4 with Roe body that came in 1950 for contract work and went to Hardwick's from September 1952 until May 1954 when the PD2 SUA296 replaced it. I have not found any pictures of 926 at Hardwick's, but it was reported when returned to WAT, to be in a brown and cream livery. Eventually painted red and cream 926 is seen with Farsley OC in June 1954 at Pudsey. It stayed with Farsley until December 1956 when it is suspected to have been scrapped.

Bought in 1953, is all Leyland RUA294 in the livery/lettering used before the 1966 change to use more cream.

The two new Leyland PD2s came in 1953/1954 and then a Roe double-decker rebodied WAT coach in 1956; this was to be the spare bus.

MUM275 when it was a WAT coach with Wilks and Meade (owned by WAT) C33F body. It had operated with the WAT Farsley operation from October 1954 until it was re-bodied when it came straight to Hardwick's.

The spare bus was MUM275 and is here sparkling new at Roes after receiving its new H61RD body. 275 entered service in May 1956 and seems to have replaced AUM433. Eventually, 275 was replaced at Hardwick's by the transfer of Farsley's HNW366D in April 1968.

MUM275 unloads in Malton on the Saturday only service with, at its side, Bedford Plaxton OB HBT880 of Milburn's from Leavening ready for the eventual return; a 20 or 35 or 40-minute timetabled journey to Leavening, dependent on the route taken.

MUM275 with rear doors and Kippax LNW869 with no doors, probably taken in 1968 when both buses were withdrawn (and are seen perhaps at the dealers Hughes). This was after the Kippax and Farsley services were taken over by Leeds City Transport without any of the buses. The extra step on the entrance on 869 can be seen, this being to enable the fitting of the patented Roe safety staircase.

The three Hardwick's double-decker buses (RUA/SUA/MUM) ran the main service until 1967/1968 when Leyland PD3s replaced them; one of these was bought new in late 1966 and the other two were transferred from Farsley. These three PD3s stayed until 1971.

HNW365D was new in November 1966 and stayed until the end, being joined by sister vehicle 366D from the Farsley fleet in 1968. Seen here in Scarborough Westwood Bus Station, it was delivered in the "more cream" livery introduced in July 1966 to the WAT stage bus fleets.

HNW366D from Farsley, with what looks like an illuminated advertising board, has just done a U-turn from Northway Bus Station and exited through Brook Street and then Trafalgar Street for Northway. It will soon work its way out of Scarborough along Westborough/the A64 and for this early start of its journey, parallels the West Yorkshire 43 route to York, Leeds and Bradford.

Full details are patchy for the single-decker vehicles operated by Hardwick's in the 1950s/early 1960s. In 1952 there were nine single-deckers, eight from Hardwick's plus in the next few years, an AEC Regal was transferred from WAT and a WAT OB came until 1955.

On the right is 1947 KUM386 that was transferred to Hardwick's from 1952 to 1955 and was then withdrawn. It saw some time with Wimpey the builders before being auctioned in 1960; it was next seen in Malta. Seemingly it was not used but has been recently discovered and is now undergoing preservation on the island!

Gradually, the original Hardwick's fleet went, apart from the Commer shown earlier. Indeed, according to records covering 1956 to 1960, the Commer seems to have been the only owned single-decker in the Hardwick's fleet. However, WAT was busy with loans from 1952 to 1958 (as the fleet list, available on request, shows) and Bedford OBs/SBs, a Leyland PS and an AEC Regal were loaned. It is also known that in 1960 and 1961, short-term transfers were made of Plaxton-bodied Commer Avengers that had been with Wallace Arnold Devon, two and then three having been recorded with Hardwick's in this period.

WAT 1949 Bedford OB MUA346 came to Hardwick's for a year from 1954 after which it was withdrawn. The Duple C29F body is unusual in not having the waistband flashing.

The stage fleet, however, did finally receive a more fixed single-decker allocation in 1961, when four 1956 Wallace Arnold Burlingham Seagull coaches came and stayed until 1965. After these, four Wallace Arnold "first edition" Plaxton Panorama coaches replaced them.

Commer/Plaxton UUB403 with WAT spent 1960 at Hardwick's and was one of five similar coaches loaned in 1960/1961.

WUM45 to 48 came over to Hardwick's and 45 is seen here when with WAT. It is coincidentally in Scarborough seafront along with a United Bristol rebuild from 1957 with ECW FDP39C bodywork for the seafront service.

WUM49 is with the Farsley fleet but is identical to WUM45 to 48 that were with Hardwick's from 1961 to 1965.

Leyland/Burlingham Seagull WAT 8338 U, sister to 8330U that spent a year at Hardwick's in 1964/1965.

Panoramas 9203 to 9206NW came in 1965 and here is 9205NW leaving Scarborough on a short to Snainton. In 1968, 9203 and 9206NW were exchanged for Farsley's Leopard 833KUA and PD3 909EUM. Meanwhile 9204/5NW stayed with Hardwick's until 1969 when they were replaced by MYJ764/765.

The two 1950s Leyland PD2s and the Daimler CVD6 double-decker went in 1967/1968 and were replaced by the three Leyland PD3s mentioned earlier that stayed until 1971. Meanwhile, Panorama 9203NW was replaced in 1968 by the Leyland Plaxton Highway bus 833KUA from the Farsley Omnibus operation in Leeds.

833KUA was another transfer from Farsley in 1968. As 1964 Leyland/Plaxton Highway dual-purpose bus it had been delivered to Farsley in the mainly red livery.

The last two Panoramas had gone by 1969 after two coaches were transferred over from the main WAT fleet. Fitted for one-man operation these stayed until 1971.

MYJ764/765 were former Dickson, Dundee AEC Reliances with Plaxton Panorama coach bodies that were new 1962 and came to WAT in 1963 when they had bought Dickson's. They came to Hardwick's in 1969 and are seen on layover in Scarborough complete with "Pay as you Enter" signage; 765 on the main route and 764 on a school special.

In 1971 full one-person-operation (OPO) was seen to be the way forward, so the three Leyland PD3 double-deckers went, along with the two ex-WAT former Dickson single-deckers. These were replaced by four AEC Swifts from Sheffield, that introduced a two-tone grey and orange livery. Hardwick's had planned to receive buses TWE20 to 23F but on collection, 23 would not start, so TWE28F came instead. An omen perhaps, as they had a habit of not starting, especially when full of passengers!

TWE21F has just arrived into Westwood, with a full looking coach park behind, including a Selnec single-decker from the Manchester area. On the left is a bus used for left luggage, the former East Yorkshire Leyland/Roe LAT69, which had the role from 1966 to March 1972.

Two of the short-lived AEC Swifts showing the two tone grey and orange livery they introduced in 1971.

In 1972 WAT transferred a 1967 Leopard with Plaxton Panorama coach body (JUA300E) and fitted it for one-man operation. It stayed with Hardwick's until 1974. JUA300E is seen here in WAT grey with Hardwick's name on the side, whilst laying over in Scarborough off a school special.

The Sheffield Swifts were, however, not successful vehicles and in 1974 they were replaced by six new KUM registered 1973 Plaxton Panorama bus grant express bodied Leylands. Initially these had been used by WAT as coaches over two seasons until 1974 when they were brought off tour work overnight and sent to Scarborough, and the Swifts came to Leeds for contract work. One report says the KUMs had done too much excursion and tour mileage to satisfy bus grant requirements and WAT had to repay; however, another report says the KUMs came perilously close to running up too much mileage on tours, so just in time, they were fitted with bus seats to replace the unreliable Swifts at Hardwick's. Eventually, when five years old, two went back in 1978 to full-time coach duties with Wallace Arnold, leaving the balance four to serve with Hardwick's until 1986. They became the oldest buses in the WAT fleet.

One of the six Leyland Leopards with Panorama Express bodies new in 1973 were KUM507 to 512L in the two-tone grey Wallace Arnold livery. Eventually painted into an orange, brown and white livery, this batch had bus grant issues. 507, 509, 511 and 512 stayed on with Hardwick's until 1986, whilst 508 and 510 were returned to WAT in 1978.

KUM510L in the unique brown, orange, brown and white livery. 510, with 508, returned to WAT in 1978 and had new coach seats fitted.

KUM511L meets United 6521 on black ice at Westwood in the winter of 1983/1984. It was renumbered 6267 in 1984 and was one of those transferred to East Yorkshire with the UAS Scarborough and Pickering depot operations in 1986. A Leyland Tiger with Plaxton Panorama Express 3200 body, it became East Yorkshire 21 and was coincidentally loaned to Hardwick's in 1987.

The KUMs were eventually replaced in 1986 by more ex-Wallace Arnold coaches, this time with four 1981 Plaxton Supreme bodies numbered PNW311/312 and 332/333W. These received new folding entrance doors as fitted on the Supreme "Express" body variant.

PNW312W loads opposite WAT Columbus Ravine depot in Scarborough for Ebberston, with a friendly lady waving at the camera!

Bus deregulation, brought in by Government, was now looming, and this dramatically changed all UK bus operations. Initially Hardwick's appeared to have embraced the change and they won a zero tender in 1986 for evenings and weekends to Pickering and Helmsley on the former United route 128. Two ex-GMB Leyland Nationals were purchased for this work. Two ex-GMB Atlanteans were also purchased in 1986, this to start a new open-top service along the Scarborough seafront competing with the incumbent operators.

NEN952R was one of the two Leyland Nationals bought from GMB in 1986 for the evening tender win on the 128 to Helmsley, and is seen here on a short to Sawdon from Scarborough where it is waiting opposite the WAT Columbus Ravine depot (note the no parking sign in red).

The Wallace Arnold Hardwick's open top bus fleet were 1972 Leyland Atlanteans WBN959L and CYC658A (originally VNB108L) that came from Greater Manchester Buses in 1986.

End Times

In late 1987 Wallace Arnold said they saw little future in bus operations and sold Hardwick's to East Yorkshire Motor Services (EYMS) on the 5th October that year. WAT had been looking at a few new ventures – in 1986, for example, they had examined operating, with Yorkshire Rider, Saturday coastal express services; this though, never passed the discussion stage. In late 1986 they won a tender for the 128 route to Helmsley but finally decided that now they were primarily a holiday tour company and made the decision to stay with this core business.

East Yorkshire went onto absorb the stage bus operation into their Scarborough and District operations which held 105 licences, with Hardwick's having a licence for 20 vehicles. The S&D subsidiary had originated in 1986 from the transfer of the former United operations, including the depots based in Vernon Road, Scarborough and at Pickering.

WAT also sold their Scarborough business to East Yorkshire. This came with eleven coaches, the WAT depot at Columbus Ravine, the WAT Beaconsfield Street workshop and the Hardwick's depot at Snainton. All these three properties were soon sold, in March 1988, by EYMS and were replaced by the existing depots at Pickering and Scarborough. The former Hardwick's Ebberston route was placed by EYMS/S&D into the 128 route to Helmsley. East Yorkshire also inherited the four Hardwick's bus PNW's and seven WAT 1981 PNW registered Plaxton Supremes coaches that were used on the former RCA contract, plus the two Hardwick's Leyland Nationals, the two WAT Atlantean open-toppers, two WAT Mercedes L508 minibuses used on the internal RCA contract and one WAT Fiat 79.14 19 seater coach.

Bus privatisation in one shot at Pickering with left to right, former East Midland and UAS Leopard/Alexander now with EYMS/Scarborough & District, former West Yorkshire Panorama Express now York & District and one of two former EY Leyland Nationals that replaced the former GMB ones with Hardwick's.

Changes continued at pace and former WAT/Hardwick's PNW311W is here at the former UAS Pickering depot.

Initially short of vehicles, East Yorkshire also had a loan from October to mid-November 1987 of three West Yorkshire Road Car Leyland Tigers with Plaxton Paramount Express bodies (2702 EWW945Y, 2402 EWW950Y & 2713 B85SWX) that were new in 1983 and 1985.

East Yorkshire 189 running on the Hardwick's route complete with tatty cardboard signboards. West Yorkshire 2702, an on loan Leyland Tiger, is just visible on the right.

One of the loaned coaches was East Yorkshire 21 when it was registered A521EVN. It had been new to UAS in 1983 and came to EYMS in the 1986 transfers. A Leyland Tiger with Plaxton Panorama Express 3200 body it stayed for two months only and was then returned to East Yorkshire and reregistered as above, in June 1988.

East Yorkshire soon transferred in two newer Leyland Nationals along with some Leyland Tigers and Leopards with Plaxton Paramount and Supreme IV bodies, some of these buses having come from the September 1986 United purchase. All these transferred coaches were painted in Hardwick's colours and a selection of them follows…

Another of the transferred coaches from East Yorkshire was a 1984 Leyland Tiger A106MKH with Plaxton Paramount 3200 body. Fleet number 6, it then went to the Scarborough & District fleet in February 1989 and in 1990 to the main fleet.

Hardwick's 26 NGR117T was new in 1979 with Plaxton Supreme IV body to United, then to East Yorkshire in 1986, Hardwick's in January 1988, Cherry in October 1988, East Yorkshire Travel in October 1992 and finally withdrawn in November 1993. It then went through eight other operators before being sold for scrap in 2003.

Hardwick's 29 NGR120T also had an interesting life. New in 1979 with Plaxton Supreme IV body to United, it was transferred to East Yorkshire in 1986 when it became East Yorkshire/Scarborough & District 230, before coming as 29 to Hardwick's in December 1987. But this was only for a short time as in October 1988 it left for another subsidiary Cherry, coming back to EYMS in 1992, then to yet another subsidiary Primrose Valley in 1993. It came back to the main fleet in 1994 where it stayed until being finally sold in December 1996.

Hardwick's 36 with Paramount 3500 body was a Leyland Tiger new in 1984 to United and came over to East Yorkshire in 1986. In December 1987 it came to Hardwick's before being sold in October 1988.

The former WAT Columbus Ravine depot is now occupied by East Yorkshire with Hardwick's name prominent and EYMS coaches in the depot. This was only for a short time as in March 1988 the premises were sold, and the fleet was then formally based at Vernon Road (the former UAS depot) before moving to Dunslow Road in February 1990.

It seems likely that Hardwick's became for a short time, the "coach arm" of the EYMS Scarborough & District operation; however, most of the coaches transferred to Hardwick's were soon withdrawn and/or were re-transferred in the early 1990s.

Three of the four former Hardwick's/WAT Plaxton Supreme "Express" buses stayed with EYMS until 1996/1997 and were repainted in the red and white Scarborough & District livery.

Hardwick's PNW312W inside the former UAS Pickering depot and is now S&D212.